Wine Tasting Journal

My wine travel experiences

Volume _____

Printed in United States of America
ISBN 978-0-9967661-0-4

TERRE
VENTURES
PUBLISHING

Journaling the Enjoyment of Wine Travels

Many of my best vacations include wine tasting especially to destinations to explore a specific wine region--Paso Robles, Sonoma, Willamette, Finger Lakes, Long Island, Virginia and Tuscany. And many more are on my list to visit and taste.

However, after so many tastings, I mix up what and where I've tasted them. I've taken notes using the tasting room sheet or a little notebook. There's no consistency. Notes are scattered about.

Most journals I tried are all about the bottle. I wanted to record my experience in the region and its wineries as well as the wine itself. So I wrote the journal I could not find.

I've found the easiest and most natural way to learn about wine is to explore a wine region. Just about every state in the US and most countries have wineries. Immerse yourself. Walk the vineyard. Eat local food. Picnic on the winery grounds.

Learn why specific grape varietals do best in the area. Although wineries may share similar growing and climate conditions, it's fun to taste how different the wines are based on each wine maker's unique style.

Plan ahead. Call for tour and tasting hours. Only visit 3 – 4 wineries a day. Allow time to relax and linger at each to get the best experience.

Many wines can only be purchased in the tasting room or through wine clubs. Be sure to bring a cooler for your car or packing material to ship, even in your checked luggage, to extend your experience at home.

I wish you endless wine pleasures—trip by trip, sip by sip!

How to Use This Journal

This journal will help you capture your tasting experience, to put into words your impressions of the wine region and winery as well as specific wines. I developed the tasting form based on my own experience. They are easy to use, not complicated or laborious.

By tasting, you learn. Describe your sensory experience and take notes using wine words. It will help you recall your experience and can place you right back there.

Be curious about the wine and the winery. The tasting room may be simple or sophisticated. The key is a knowledgeable pourer who will tell you the story of the founder, the vineyard and each wine. If not, don't hesitate to ask about it. A compelling story adds a dimension of understanding and appreciation for the wine. We remember stories. Telling it again can be a fun way of sharing your experience.

Keeping a wine journal is a gift to yourself. I encourage you to use it often. Fill this journal up. Buy another and another as you travel about. Mark the volume number on the title page and even on the spine with a marker.

You'll have a wonderful history of your enjoyable travels—and you will see how your palate has developed and your experiences broadened.

"Quickly, bring me a beaker of wine, so
that I may wet my mind and say
something clever."
~ *Aristophanes* ~

This journal is not a comprehensive education. There are plenty of expert books and classes for that. I've given you just enough information, gleaned from many of those experts, to give you the words to describe the taste, smell, and experience.

The first part is a **short reference** to help you describe the wine. Use this section when writing your notes.

- **Wine Speak**, common words to describe wine and help you understand what the sommelier is explaining.

- **Tasting Etiquette**, the art of wine tasting using the S's – See, Swirl, Sniff, Sip, Spit, Savor.

- **Wine Characteristics,** a fairly comprehensive listing of aromas, tastes, and flavors commonly found in various Red, White and Rosé wines to help you put words to your impression of the wine. If the wine you are drinking is not on the list, simply look at other red or white wines for descriptors to use. Book mark this section to reference when tasting.

Part two is the **Tasting Notes**. This section includes:

- **Personal Table of Contents**, where you create your own chapters for each Wine Region you visit

- **Wine Region,** record your impression of up to 3 regions

- **Winery**, your impressions of the winery, tour, and tasting room

- **Tasting Notes**, 8 wines per winery, guided sections to make it easy to record color, aroma, overall deliciousness and more

- **Blank Tasting Notes**, 16 additional pages for other wines tasted

Wine Speak

Can't find the right word to describe the wine you're drinking? You're not alone. There is so much wine terminology you can feel like you're listening to a foreign language.

To not overwhelm you, I've chosen just a few of the most common and useful definitions of wine characteristics. If you want more advanced terminology, just search the internet or pick up a wine education book.

Acidity – a taste sensation of sourness, like lemon or vinegar, perceived most vividly along the sides of the tongue. High acidity gives the impression of freshness, crisp, lively, or sharp. Low acidity is often referred to as soft. Acidity is more a taste factor in white wines.

Aroma or Bouquet – an olfactory sensation or smell of a wine. Also called the 'nose' of the wine. Bouquet is the complex aroma in more aged wines.

Balance – one of the most desired characteristics, the concentration of fruit, tannin, and acidity are in total harmony.

Body – the tactile sensation of weight or thickness on the palate, increases with wine's alcohol content. You can classify it as light, medium, or full bodied.

Complexity – wines projecting multi-faceted aromas or flavors. A complex wine is interesting to drink, carrying a variety of subtle flavors and scents from the first sip to long after swallowing.

Finish – the lingering impression or aftertaste of wine that stays in the back of your mouth and throat after it is swallowed. Typically, the longer a pleasant finish lasts, the better the wine quality.

Fruit – an umbrella term for aromas and flavors that come from grapes and their fermentation. A wine is often characterized by their main fruit flavors. Red wines are associated with red or dark fruits like raspberry or blackberry whereas white wines are more citrus, peach, or apple flavors.

Sweet / Dry – a taste sensation at the tip of your tongue, perceived as sweet when not all grape sugar has been converted to alcohol. Most often described in terms of its opposite, the lack of perceptible sweetness called 'dryness.'

Tannin – an astringent compound found in grape skins and stems, extracted during fermentation and aging. Only found in red wines. Depending on the amount, you might describe it as astringent, firm, soft, or mellow. A high tannin wine may taste bitter on the sides of your tongue. It can make your tongue feel dry. But don't confuse this with the wine being 'dry' simply because your mouth dries out.

"Wine makes daily living easier, less hurried, with fewer tensions and more tolerance."
~ *Benjamin Franklin* ~

Tasting Etiquette

Wine tasting is different from drinking a glass of wine.

Tasting is a slower process where you learn about the wine, often multiple wines. You put words to the wine.

Drinking, you enjoy a glass or bottle of wine, often along with food and conversation.

When drinking, comments about the wine are part of the conversation.

In tasting, **it *is* the conversation**.

During the tasting, you'll be describing the aromas, flavors, and textures of the wine. As your knowledge grows, you'll soon understand why the flavors exist in the wine based on conditions such as how ripe the grapes were when picked, were they aged in steel or barrels, whether a wine is young or aged, what the winemaker likes. Be sure to get the story behind the style.

Pay attention at each step. Take notes. And most importantly - *enjoy!*

"Wine is bottled poetry."
~ *Robert Louis Stevenson* ~

The "S's" of Wine Tasting Etiquette

See: Pour wine into glass. Observe against a white surface. Study the color. Look for clarity and brilliance.

Swirl: Take initial sniff, then hold stem (not bowl) and lightly swirl wine around. Allow it to breathe and release its aroma.

Sniff: Raise glass to your nose. Inhale deeply. Use the characteristics chart to record your initial aroma impression.

Sip: Allow wine to move over and under your tongue to reach all taste buds. Draw in a bit of air to carry the aroma to your olfactory glands. Hold in your mouth before swallowing. Take note of fruit, spice, dry, sweet, tannin, acidity. Was taste different from the nose?

Spit: Alternative to actually swallowing more than a tiny sip. It may seem gauche but perfectly acceptable in tasting circles. It allows you to maximize the number of wines you taste without embarrassing circumstances and helps prevent palate fatigue which sadly can happen.

Savor: Flavors don't end when you swallow. Check for balance. Notice the body and finish.

"A bottle of wine contains more philosophy
than all the books in the world."
~ Louis Pasteur ~

Red Wine Characteristics

Pinot Noir
Rhubarb
Raspberry
Black Cherry
Blackberry
Plum
Violet
Wilted Rose
Dark chocolate
Plum
Earthy
Rock minerality
Beet
Tree bark
Forest floor
Moss
Cola
Tar
Prune
Spice

Shiraz/Syrah
Black olive
Pepper
Spice
Raspberry
Blackberry
Red currant
Cherry
Plum
Violet
Anise
Cassis
Caramel
Chocolate
Leather
Soy

Zinfandel
Cedar
Raspberry
Spice
Pepper
Blackberry
Blackcurrant
Plum
Fruitcake
Cinnamon
Strawberry
Walnut cola
Raisin
Tar
Earthy
Caramel
Dark chocolate
Leather

Grenache
Pepper
Spice
Anise
Caraway
Raspberry
Black cherry
Prune
Blackberry
Plum
Orange peel
Gamey
Earthy
Mineral

Cabernet Sauvignon
Boysenberry
Cherry
Blackberry
Black currant
Plum
Fig
Anise
Violet
Raspberry
Clove
Sage
Thyme
Dark chocolate
Sassafras
Cedar
Black olive
Green pepper
Loamy earth
Cigar box
Coffee
Smoke
Beet

Red Wine Characteristics

Merlot
Sappy
Black olive
Sage
Strawberry
Raspberry
Anise
Spice
Cherry
Plum
Violet
Blackberry
Guava
Blackcurrant
Beet
Fruitcake
Coffee
Tobacco
Wet earth

Cabernet Franc
Tarragon
Dusty
Cherry
Blackberry
Plum
Violet
Mint
Musk
Mineral
Pencil shavings
Tobacco

Sangiovese
Rhubarb
Caper
Raspberry
Sour cherry
Plum
Pine
Prune
Strawberry
Spice
Perfumed
Tobacco
Smoke
Anise
Red currant

Tempranillo
Herbal
Raspberry
Cherry
Blackberry
Cinnamon
Chocolate
Anise
Pine
Prune
Clove
Leather
Balsamic
Tobacco
Smoke

Chianti
Black cherry
Plum
Blackberry
Raspberry
Vanilla
Spice
Leather
Earth
Tobacco
Tar

White Wine Characteristics

Chardonnay
Cucumber
Celery
Mineral
Green apple
Grapefruit
Vanilla
Lemon
Lime
Honey
Nectarine
Pineapple
Peach
Melon
Tangerine
Oak
Cream
Brioche
Toast
Almond
Butter
Pear

Viogner
Orange blossom
Violet
Floral
Hay
Mango
Lychee
Smoky tea
Melon
Pear
Peach
Apricot
Grapefruit
Honeysuckle

Pinot Gris
Rose
Violet
Floral
Lychee
Apple
Pear
Nectarine
Melon
Peach
Lemon
Butter
Grapefruit
Quince
Saffron
Jasmine

Sauvignon Blanc
Boxwood
Tomato bush
Celery
Candied ginger
Asparagus
Artichoke
Green bean
Pea pod
Cut grass
Lemon verbena
Lemongrass
Lime zest
Peach
Gooseberry
Grapefruit
Melon
Tropical fruit
Mineral
Flint – wet stone

Riesling
Mineral
Herbal
Slate
Grapefruit
Lemon curd
Lime
Orange peel
Rose
Jasmine
Honeysuckle
Bath salts
Cold cream
Apple
Pear
Pineapple
Peach
Apricot
Nectarine
Honey
Pine nut
Green tea

Chenin Blanc
Cut grass
Apricot
Green apple
Citrus
Hay
Peach
Quince
Spice

White Wine and Rosé Characteristics

Gewurztraminer	Semillion	Rosé
Grapefruit	Lantana	Almond
Perfumed	Asparagus	Rose water
Banana	Green bean	Violet
Cold cream	Pea pod	Peach flower
Rose	Gooseberry	Wild flowers
Musk	Cut grass	Peony
Lavender	Green apple	Jasmine
Potpourri	Lemongrass	Freesia
Bitter almond	Lemon	Orange blossom
Thai basil	Orange	Watermelon
Melon	Hay	Lime
Lychee	Pear	White Cherry
Passionfruit	Pineapple	Strawberry
Peach	Marmalade	Raspberry
Pineapple	Quince	Peach
Apricot	Fig	Black currant
Honey	Honey	Blackberry
Clove	Biscuit	Banana
Spice	Toast	Apple
Smoke	Smoke	Plum
Tropical fruit	Flint	Pear
	Hazelnut	Blueberry
	Almond	Apricot
	Butter	Kiwi
	Saffron	Mango
		Pomegranate
		Orange
		Tangerine
		Grapefruit
		Lychee
		Pineapple
		Cinnamon
		Wet stone

"A bottle of wine begs to be shared;
I have never met a miserly wine lover."
~ *Clifton Fadiman* ~

My Wine Travels

Volume _____

Wine Region .... Date ....…..

Wine Region .... Date ....…..

Wine Region .... Date ....…...

Wine Region _____

Sketch or attach printed map of region:

Wine Region _____

Wineries and Wine Tasting Notes on pages _____

Overall impression of region:

....

....

....

....

....

Travel Companions: ....

....

Hotel: ....

Restaurants: ....

....

....

Future Visits:

Additional Wineries to visit: ....

....

....

Places to stay: ....

....

Places to eat: ....

....

Other recommendations: ....

....

Wine Region _____

Sketch or attach printed map of region:

Wine Region _____

Wineries and Wine Tasting Notes on pages _____

Overall impression of region:

....

....

....

....

....

Travel Companions: ....

....

Hotel: ....

Restaurants: ....

....

....

Future Visits:

Additional Wineries to visit: ....

....

....

Places to stay: ....

....

Places to eat: ....

....

Other recommendations: ....

....

Wine Region _____

Sketch or attach printed map of region:

Wine Region _____

Wineries and Wine Tasting Notes on pages _____

Overall impression of region:

....

....

....

....

....

Travel Companions: ....

....

Hotel: ....

Restaurants: ....

....

....

Future Visits:

Additional Wineries to visit: ....

....

....

Places to stay: ....

....

Places to eat: ....

....

Other recommendations: ....

....

Winery _____ Region_____

Winery Tour Experience

Appointment / reservation required? Y / N

Winery recommended by: ....

Winery Story: ....

....

....

....

....

....

Key information learned: ....

....

....

....

Tasting Room Experience

Appointment / reservation required? Y / N

Cost of tasting: .... Name of Pourer ....

Description of tasting room: ....

....

....

....

....

Recommendations for future visits: ....

....

....

Tasting Notes

Winery _____   Date _____
Name of Wine _____   Vintage _____
Varietal _____   Bottle Price _____

Aroma Notes:	Tasting Notes:

Hint: Use Wine Characteristics Chart

Color:

	Maroon
	Garnet
	Ruby
	Fuchsia
	Salmon
	Peach
	Amber
	Gold
	Straw

Overall Impression:

Pairing Ideas:

Fill wine glasses for
Deliciousness
Rating:

Tasting Notes

Winery _____   Date _____

Name of Wine _____   Vintage _____

Varietal _____   Bottle Price _____

Aroma Notes:	Tasting Notes:

Hint: Use Wine Characteristics Chart

Color:

	Maroon
	Garnet
	Ruby
	Fuchsia
	Salmon
	Peach
	Amber
	Gold
	Straw

Overall Impression:

Pairing Ideas:

Fill wine glasses for
Deliciousness
Rating:

Tasting Notes

Winery _____   Date _____
Name of Wine _____   Vintage _____
Varietal _____   Bottle Price _____

Aroma Notes:	Tasting Notes:

Hint: Use Wine Characteristics Chart

Color:

- Maroon
- Garnet
- Ruby
- Fuchsia
- Salmon
- Peach
- Amber
- Gold
- Straw

Overall Impression:

Pairing Ideas:

Fill wine glasses for
Deliciousness
Rating:

Tasting Notes

Winery _____   Date _____
Name of Wine _____   Vintage _____
Varietal _____   Bottle Price _____

Aroma Notes:	Tasting Notes:

Hint: Use Wine Characteristics Chart

Color:

- Maroon
- Garnet
- Ruby
- Fuchsia
- Salmon
- Peach
- Amber
- Gold
- Straw

Overall Impression:

Pairing Ideas:

Fill wine glasses for Deliciousness Rating:

Tasting Notes

Winery _____ Date _____
Name of Wine _____ Vintage _____
Varietal _____ Bottle Price _____

Aroma Notes:	Tasting Notes:

Hint: Use Wine Characteristics Chart

Color:

- Maroon
- Garnet
- Ruby
- Fuchsia
- Salmon
- Peach
- Amber
- Gold
- Straw

Overall Impression:

Pairing Ideas:

Fill wine glasses for
Deliciousness
Rating:

Tasting Notes

Winery _____   Date _____
Name of Wine _____   Vintage _____
Varietal _____   Bottle Price _____

Aroma Notes:	Tasting Notes:

Hint: Use Wine Characteristics Chart

Color:

- Maroon
- Garnet
- Ruby
- Fuchsia
- Salmon
- Peach
- Amber
- Gold
- Straw

Overall Impression:

Pairing Ideas:

Fill wine glasses for
Deliciousness
Rating:

Tasting Notes

Winery _____   Date _____
Name of Wine _____   Vintage _____
Varietal _____   Bottle Price _____

Aroma Notes:	Tasting Notes:

Hint: Use Wine Characteristics Chart

Color:

Maroon

Garnet

Ruby

Fuchsia

Salmon

Peach

Amber

Gold

Straw

Overall Impression:

Pairing Ideas:

Fill wine glasses for
Deliciousness
Rating:

Tasting Notes

Winery _____   Date _____

Name of Wine _____   Vintage _____

Varietal _____   Bottle Price _____

Aroma Notes:	Tasting Notes:

Hint: Use Wine Characteristics Chart

Color:

- Maroon
- Garnet
- Ruby
- Fuchsia
- Salmon
- Peach
- Amber
- Gold
- Straw

Overall Impression:

Pairing Ideas:

Fill wine glasses for
Deliciousness
Rating:

Winery _____ Region_____

Winery Tour Experience

Appointment / reservation required? Y / N

Winery recommended by: ....

Winery Story: ....

....

....

....

....

....

Key information learned: ....

....

....

....

Tasting Room Experience

Appointment / reservation required? Y / N

Cost of tasting: .... Name of Pourer ....

Description of tasting room: ....

....

....

....

....

Recommendations for future visits: ....

....

....

Tasting Notes

Winery _____   Date _____
Name of Wine _____   Vintage _____
Varietal _____   Bottle Price _____

Aroma Notes:	Tasting Notes:

Hint: Use Wine Characteristics Chart

Color:

Maroon

Garnet

Ruby

Fuchsia

Salmon

Peach

Amber

Gold

Straw

Overall Impression:

Pairing Ideas:

Fill wine glasses for
Deliciousness
Rating:

Tasting Notes

Winery _____   Date _____
Name of Wine _____   Vintage _____
Varietal _____   Bottle Price _____

Aroma Notes:	Tasting Notes:

Hint: Use Wine Characteristics Chart

Color:

Maroon

Garnet

Ruby

Fuchsia

Salmon

Peach

Amber

Gold

Straw

Overall Impression:

Pairing Ideas:

Fill wine glasses for
Deliciousness
Rating:

Tasting Notes

Winery _____   Date _____
Name of Wine _____   Vintage _____
Varietal _____   Bottle Price _____

Aroma Notes:	Tasting Notes:

Hint: Use Wine Characteristics Chart

Color:

Maroon

Garnet

Ruby

Fuchsia

Salmon

Peach

Amber

Gold

Straw

Overall Impression:

Pairing Ideas:

Fill wine glasses for
Deliciousness
Rating:

Tasting Notes

Winery _____   Date _____

Name of Wine _____   Vintage _____

Varietal _____   Bottle Price _____

Aroma Notes:	Tasting Notes:

Hint: Use Wine Characteristics Chart

Color:

	Maroon
	Garnet
	Ruby
	Fuchsia
	Salmon
	Peach
	Amber
	Gold
	Straw

Overall Impression:

Pairing Ideas:

Fill wine glasses for Deliciousness Rating:

Tasting Notes

Winery _____   Date _____

Name of Wine _____   Vintage _____

Varietal _____   Bottle Price _____

Aroma Notes:	Tasting Notes:

Hint: Use Wine Characteristics Chart

Color:

- Maroon
- Garnet
- Ruby
- Fuchsia
- Salmon
- Peach
- Amber
- Gold
- Straw

Overall Impression:

Pairing Ideas:

Fill wine glasses for
Deliciousness
Rating:

Tasting Notes

Winery _____   Date _____
Name of Wine _____   Vintage _____
Varietal _____   Bottle Price _____

Aroma Notes:	Tasting Notes:

Hint: Use Wine Characteristics Chart

Color:

	Maroon
	Garnet
	Ruby
	Fuchsia
	Salmon
	Peach
	Amber
	Gold
	Straw

Overall Impression:

Pairing Ideas:

Fill wine glasses for
Deliciousness
Rating:

Tasting Notes

Winery _____   Date _____

Name of Wine _____   Vintage _____

Varietal _____   Bottle Price _____

Aroma Notes:	Tasting Notes:

Hint: Use Wine Characteristics Chart

Color:

	Maroon
	Garnet
	Ruby
	Fuchsia
	Salmon
	Peach
	Amber
	Gold
	Straw

Overall Impression:

Pairing Ideas:

Fill wine glasses for Deliciousness Rating:

Tasting Notes

Winery _____   Date _____
Name of Wine _____   Vintage _____
Varietal _____   Bottle Price _____

Aroma Notes:	Tasting Notes:

Hint: Use Wine Characteristics Chart

Color:

	Maroon
	Garnet
	Ruby
	Fuchsia
	Salmon
	Peach
	Amber
	Gold
	Straw

Overall Impression:

Pairing Ideas:

Fill wine glasses for
Deliciousness
Rating:

Winery _____ Region_____

Winery Tour Experience

Appointment / reservation required? Y / N

Winery recommended by: ....

Winery Story: ....

....

....

....

....

....

Key information learned: ....

....

....

....

Tasting Room Experience

Appointment / reservation required? Y / N

Cost of tasting: .... Name of Pourer ....

Description of tasting room: ....

....

....

....

....

Recommendations for future visits: ....

....

....

Tasting Notes

Winery _____   Date _____
Name of Wine _____   Vintage _____
Varietal _____   Bottle Price _____

Aroma Notes:	Tasting Notes:

Hint: Use Wine Characteristics Chart

Color:

- Maroon
- Garnet
- Ruby
- Fuchsia
- Salmon
- Peach
- Amber
- Gold
- Straw

Overall Impression:

Pairing Ideas:

Fill wine glasses for
Deliciousness
Rating:

Tasting Notes

Winery _____ Date _____
Name of Wine _____ Vintage _____
Varietal _____ Bottle Price _____

Aroma Notes:	Tasting Notes:

Hint: Use Wine Characteristics Chart

Color:

- Maroon
- Garnet
- Ruby
- Fuchsia
- Salmon
- Peach
- Amber
- Gold
- Straw

Overall Impression:

Pairing Ideas:

Fill wine glasses for
Deliciousness
Rating:

Tasting Notes

Winery _____   Date _____
Name of Wine _____   Vintage _____
Varietal _____   Bottle Price _____

Aroma Notes:	Tasting Notes:

Hint: Use Wine Characteristics Chart

Color:

Maroon

Garnet

Ruby

Fuchsia

Salmon

Peach

Amber

Gold

Straw

Overall Impression:

Pairing Ideas:

Fill wine glasses for
Deliciousness
Rating:

Tasting Notes

Winery _____   Date _____

Name of Wine _____   Vintage _____

Varietal _____   Bottle Price _____

Aroma Notes:	Tasting Notes:

Hint: Use Wine Characteristics Chart

Color:

- Maroon
- Garnet
- Ruby
- Fuchsia
- Salmon
- Peach
- Amber
- Gold
- Straw

Overall Impression:

Pairing Ideas:

Fill wine glasses for
Deliciousness
Rating:

Tasting Notes

Winery _____   Date _____
Name of Wine _____   Vintage _____
Varietal _____   Bottle Price _____

Aroma Notes:	Tasting Notes:

Hint: Use Wine Characteristics Chart

Color:

Overall Impression:

	Maroon
	Garnet
	Ruby
	Fuchsia
	Salmon
	Peach
	Amber
	Gold
	Straw

Pairing Ideas:

Fill wine glasses for
Deliciousness
Rating:

Tasting Notes

Winery _____   Date _____
Name of Wine _____   Vintage _____
Varietal _____   Bottle Price _____

Aroma Notes:	Tasting Notes:

Hint: Use Wine Characteristics Chart

Color:

- Maroon
- Garnet
- Ruby
- Fuchsia
- Salmon
- Peach
- Amber
- Gold
- Straw

Overall Impression:

Pairing Ideas:

Fill wine glasses for
Deliciousness
Rating:

Tasting Notes

Winery _____   Date _____
Name of Wine _____   Vintage _____
Varietal _____   Bottle Price _____

Aroma Notes:	Tasting Notes:

Hint: Use Wine Characteristics Chart

Color:

- Maroon
- Garnet
- Ruby
- Fuchsia
- Salmon
- Peach
- Amber
- Gold
- Straw

Overall Impression:

Pairing Ideas:

Fill wine glasses for
Deliciousness
Rating:

Tasting Notes

Winery _____   Date _____

Name of Wine _____   Vintage _____

Varietal _____   Bottle Price _____

Aroma Notes:	Tasting Notes:

Hint: Use Wine Characteristics Chart

Color:

	Overall Impression:
Maroon	
Garnet	
Ruby	
Fuchsia	
Salmon	
Peach	Pairing Ideas:
Amber	
Gold	
Straw	

Fill wine glasses for
Deliciousness
Rating:

Winery _____ Region_____

Winery Tour Experience

Appointment / reservation required? Y / N

Winery recommended by: ....

Winery Story: ....

....

....

....

....

....

Key information learned: ....

....

....

....

Tasting Room Experience

Appointment / reservation required? Y / N

Cost of tasting: .... Name of Pourer ....

Description of tasting room: ....

....

....

....

....

Recommendations for future visits: ....

....

....

Tasting Notes

Winery _____   Date _____
Name of Wine _____   Vintage _____
Varietal _____   Bottle Price _____

Aroma Notes:	Tasting Notes:

Hint: Use Wine Characteristics Chart

Color:

Maroon

Garnet

Ruby

Fuchsia

Salmon

Peach

Amber

Gold

Straw

Overall Impression:

Pairing Ideas:

Fill wine glasses for
Deliciousness
Rating:

Tasting Notes

Winery _____   Date _____
Name of Wine _____   Vintage _____
Varietal _____   Bottle Price _____

Aroma Notes:	Tasting Notes:

Hint: Use Wine Characteristics Chart

Color:

- Maroon
- Garnet
- Ruby
- Fuchsia
- Salmon
- Peach
- Amber
- Gold
- Straw

Overall Impression:

Pairing Ideas:

Fill wine glasses for
Deliciousness
Rating:

Tasting Notes

Winery _____   Date _____
Name of Wine _____   Vintage _____
Varietal _____   Bottle Price _____

Aroma Notes:	Tasting Notes:

Hint: Use Wine Characteristics Chart

Color:

- Maroon
- Garnet
- Ruby
- Fuchsia
- Salmon
- Peach
- Amber
- Gold
- Straw

Overall Impression:

Pairing Ideas:

Fill wine glasses for
Deliciousness
Rating:

Tasting Notes

Winery _____   Date _____
Name of Wine _____   Vintage _____
Varietal _____   Bottle Price _____

Aroma Notes:	Tasting Notes:

Hint: Use Wine Characteristics Chart

Color:

Maroon

Garnet

Ruby

Fuchsia

Salmon

Peach

Amber

Gold

Straw

Overall Impression:

Pairing Ideas:

Fill wine glasses for
Deliciousness
Rating:

Tasting Notes

Winery _____ Date _____

Name of Wine _____ Vintage _____

Varietal _____ Bottle Price _____

Aroma Notes:	Tasting Notes:

Hint: Use Wine Characteristics Chart

Color:

- Maroon
- Garnet
- Ruby
- Fuchsia
- Salmon
- Peach
- Amber
- Gold
- Straw

Overall Impression:

Pairing Ideas:

Fill wine glasses for
Deliciousness
Rating:

Tasting Notes

Winery _____   Date _____
Name of Wine _____   Vintage _____
Varietal _____   Bottle Price _____

Aroma Notes:	Tasting Notes:

Hint: Use Wine Characteristics Chart

Color:

- Maroon
- Garnet
- Ruby
- Fuchsia
- Salmon
- Peach
- Amber
- Gold
- Straw

Overall Impression:

Pairing Ideas:

Fill wine glasses for
Deliciousness
Rating:

Tasting Notes

Winery _____   Date _____
Name of Wine _____   Vintage _____
Varietal _____   Bottle Price _____

Aroma Notes:	Tasting Notes:

Hint: Use Wine Characteristics Chart

Color:

- Maroon
- Garnet
- Ruby
- Fuchsia
- Salmon
- Peach
- Amber
- Gold
- Straw

Overall Impression:

Pairing Ideas:

Fill wine glasses for Deliciousness Rating:

Tasting Notes

Winery _____   Date _____
Name of Wine _____   Vintage _____
Varietal _____   Bottle Price _____

Aroma Notes:	Tasting Notes:

Hint: Use Wine Characteristics Chart

Color:

- Maroon
- Garnet
- Ruby
- Fuchsia
- Salmon
- Peach
- Amber
- Gold
- Straw

Overall Impression:

Pairing Ideas:

Fill wine glasses for
Deliciousness
Rating:

Winery _____ Region_____

Winery Tour Experience

Appointment / reservation required? Y / N

Winery recommended by: ....

Winery Story: ....

....

....

....

....

....

Key information learned: ....

....

....

....

Tasting Room Experience

Appointment / reservation required? Y / N

Cost of tasting: .... Name of Pourer ....

Description of tasting room: ....

....

....

....

....

Recommendations for future visits: ....

....

....

Tasting Notes

Winery _____   Date _____
Name of Wine _____   Vintage _____
Varietal _____   Bottle Price _____

Aroma Notes:	Tasting Notes:

Hint: Use Wine Characteristics Chart

Color:

Maroon

Garnet

Ruby

Fuchsia

Salmon

Peach

Amber

Gold

Straw

Overall Impression:

Pairing Ideas:

Fill wine glasses for
Deliciousness
Rating:

Tasting Notes

Winery _____   Date _____
Name of Wine _____   Vintage _____
Varietal _____   Bottle Price _____

Aroma Notes:	Tasting Notes:

Hint: Use Wine Characteristics Chart

Color:

Maroon

Garnet

Ruby

Fuchsia

Salmon

Peach

Amber

Gold

Straw

Overall Impression:

Pairing Ideas:

Fill wine glasses for
Deliciousness
Rating:

Tasting Notes

Winery _____   Date _____
Name of Wine _____   Vintage _____
Varietal _____   Bottle Price _____

Aroma Notes:	Tasting Notes:

Hint: Use Wine Characteristics Chart

Color:

Maroon

Garnet

Ruby

Fuchsia

Salmon

Peach

Amber

Gold

Straw

Overall Impression:

Pairing Ideas:

Fill wine glasses for
Deliciousness
Rating:

Tasting Notes

Winery _____   Date _____
Name of Wine _____   Vintage _____
Varietal _____   Bottle Price _____

Aroma Notes:	Tasting Notes:

Hint: Use Wine Characteristics Chart

Color:

- Maroon
- Garnet
- Ruby
- Fuchsia
- Salmon
- Peach
- Amber
- Gold
- Straw

Overall Impression:

Pairing Ideas:

Fill wine glasses for
Deliciousness
Rating:

Tasting Notes

Winery _____   Date _____

Name of Wine _____   Vintage _____

Varietal _____   Bottle Price _____

Aroma Notes:	Tasting Notes:

Hint: Use Wine Characteristics Chart

Color:

- Maroon
- Garnet
- Ruby
- Fuchsia
- Salmon
- Peach
- Amber
- Gold
- Straw

Overall Impression:

Pairing Ideas:

Fill wine glasses for Deliciousness Rating:

Tasting Notes

Winery _____   Date _____
Name of Wine _____   Vintage _____
Varietal _____   Bottle Price _____

Aroma Notes:	Tasting Notes:

Hint: Use Wine Characteristics Chart

Color:

	Maroon
	Garnet
	Ruby
	Fuchsia
	Salmon
	Peach
	Amber
	Gold
	Straw

Overall Impression:

Pairing Ideas:

Fill wine glasses for
Deliciousness
Rating:

Tasting Notes

Winery _____   Date _____
Name of Wine _____   Vintage _____
Varietal _____   Bottle Price _____

Aroma Notes:	Tasting Notes:

Hint: Use Wine Characteristics Chart

Color:

	Maroon
	Garnet
	Ruby
	Fuchsia
	Salmon
	Peach
	Amber
	Gold
	Straw

Overall Impression:

Pairing Ideas:

Fill wine glasses for
Deliciousness
Rating:

Tasting Notes

Winery _____   Date _____
Name of Wine _____   Vintage _____
Varietal _____   Bottle Price _____

Aroma Notes:	Tasting Notes:

Hint: Use Wine Characteristics Chart

Color:

Maroon

Garnet

Ruby

Fuchsia

Salmon

Peach

Amber

Gold

Straw

Overall Impression:

Pairing Ideas:

Fill wine glasses for
Deliciousness
Rating:

Winery _____ *Region* _____

Winery Tour Experience

Appointment / reservation required? Y / N

Winery recommended by: ....

Winery Story: ....

....

....

....

....

....

Key information learned: ....

....

....

....

Tasting Room Experience

Appointment / reservation required? Y / N

Cost of tasting: .... Name of Pourer ....

Description of tasting room: ....

....

....

....

....

Recommendations for future visits: ....

....

....

Tasting Notes

Winery _____   Date _____
Name of Wine _____   Vintage _____
Varietal _____   Bottle Price _____

Aroma Notes:	Tasting Notes:

Hint: Use Wine Characteristics Chart

Color:

Maroon

Garnet

Ruby

Fuchsia

Salmon

Peach

Amber

Gold

Straw

Overall Impression:

Pairing Ideas:

Fill wine glasses for
Deliciousness
Rating:

Tasting Notes

Winery _____   Date _____

Name of Wine _____   Vintage _____

Varietal _____   Bottle Price _____

Aroma Notes:	Tasting Notes:

Hint: Use Wine Characteristics Chart

Color:

Overall Impression:

- Maroon
- Garnet
- Ruby
- Fuchsia
- Salmon
- Peach
- Amber
- Gold
- Straw

Pairing Ideas:

Fill wine glasses for
Deliciousness
Rating:

Tasting Notes

Winery _____   Date _____

Name of Wine _____   Vintage _____

Varietal _____   Bottle Price _____

Aroma Notes:	Tasting Notes:

Hint: Use Wine Characteristics Chart

Color:

	Maroon
	Garnet
	Ruby
	Fuchsia
	Salmon
	Peach
	Amber
	Gold
	Straw

Overall Impression:

Pairing Ideas:

Fill wine glasses for
Deliciousness
Rating:

Tasting Notes

Winery _____   Date _____
Name of Wine _____   Vintage _____
Varietal _____   Bottle Price _____

Aroma Notes:	Tasting Notes:

Hint: Use Wine Characteristics Chart

Color:

- Maroon
- Garnet
- Ruby
- Fuchsia
- Salmon
- Peach
- Amber
- Gold
- Straw

Overall Impression:

Pairing Ideas:

Fill wine glasses for
Deliciousness
Rating:

Tasting Notes

Winery _____   Date _____
Name of Wine _____   Vintage _____
Varietal _____   Bottle Price _____

Aroma Notes:	Tasting Notes:

Hint: Use Wine Characteristics Chart

Color:

- Maroon
- Garnet
- Ruby
- Fuchsia
- Salmon
- Peach
- Amber
- Gold
- Straw

Overall Impression:

Pairing Ideas:

Fill wine glasses for
Deliciousness
Rating:

Tasting Notes

Winery _____   Date _____
Name of Wine _____   Vintage _____
Varietal _____   Bottle Price _____

Aroma Notes:	Tasting Notes:

Hint: Use Wine Characteristics Chart

Color:

	Maroon
	Garnet
	Ruby
	Fuchsia
	Salmon
	Peach
	Amber
	Gold
	Straw

Overall Impression:

Pairing Ideas:

Fill wine glasses for
Deliciousness
Rating:

Tasting Notes

Winery _____   Date _____
Name of Wine _____   Vintage _____
Varietal _____   Bottle Price _____

Aroma Notes:	Tasting Notes:

Hint: Use Wine Characteristics Chart

Color:

Maroon

Garnet

Ruby

Fuchsia

Salmon

Peach

Amber

Gold

Straw

Overall Impression:

Pairing Ideas:

Fill wine glasses for
Deliciousness
Rating:

Tasting Notes

Winery _____   Date _____
Name of Wine _____   Vintage _____
Varietal _____   Bottle Price _____

Aroma Notes:	Tasting Notes:

Hint: Use Wine Characteristics Chart

Color:

Overall Impression:

| Maroon |
| Garnet |
| Ruby |
| Fuchsia |
| Salmon |
| Peach |
| Amber |
| Gold |
| Straw |

Pairing Ideas:

Fill wine glasses for
Deliciousness
Rating:

Winery _____ *Region*_____

Winery Tour Experience

Appointment / reservation required? Y / N

Winery recommended by: ....

Winery Story: ....

....

....

....

....

....

Key information learned: ....

....

....

....

Tasting Room Experience

Appointment / reservation required? Y / N

Cost of tasting: .... Name of Pourer ....

Description of tasting room: ....

....

....

....

....

Recommendations for future visits: ....

....

....

Tasting Notes

Winery _____   Date _____
Name of Wine _____   Vintage _____
Varietal _____   Bottle Price _____

Aroma Notes:	Tasting Notes:

Hint: Use Wine Characteristics Chart

Color:

	Maroon
	Garnet
	Ruby
	Fuchsia
	Salmon
	Peach
	Amber
	Gold
	Straw

Overall Impression:

Pairing Ideas:

Fill wine glasses for Deliciousness Rating:

Tasting Notes

Winery _____   Date _____
Name of Wine _____   Vintage _____
Varietal _____   Bottle Price _____

Aroma Notes:	Tasting Notes:

Hint: Use Wine Characteristics Chart

Color:

Maroon

Garnet

Ruby

Fuchsia

Salmon

Peach

Amber

Gold

Straw

Overall Impression:

Pairing Ideas:

Fill wine glasses for
Deliciousness
Rating:

Tasting Notes

Winery _____   Date _____
Name of Wine _____   Vintage _____
Varietal _____   Bottle Price _____

Aroma Notes:	Tasting Notes:

Hint: Use Wine Characteristics Chart

Color:

	Maroon
	Garnet
	Ruby
	Fuchsia
	Salmon
	Peach
	Amber
	Gold
	Straw

Overall Impression:

Pairing Ideas:

Fill wine glasses for
Deliciousness
Rating:

Tasting Notes

Winery _____   Date _____

Name of Wine _____   Vintage _____

Varietal _____   Bottle Price _____

Aroma Notes:	Tasting Notes:

Hint: Use Wine Characteristics Chart

Color:

	Maroon
	Garnet
	Ruby
	Fuchsia
	Salmon
	Peach
	Amber
	Gold
	Straw

Overall Impression:

Pairing Ideas:

Fill wine glasses for
Deliciousness
Rating:

Tasting Notes

Winery _____   Date _____
Name of Wine _____   Vintage _____
Varietal _____   Bottle Price _____

Aroma Notes:	Tasting Notes:

Hint: Use Wine Characteristics Chart

Color:

Maroon

Garnet

Ruby

Fuchsia

Salmon

Peach

Amber

Gold

Straw

Overall Impression:

Pairing Ideas:

Fill wine glasses for
Deliciousness
Rating:

Tasting Notes

Winery _____   Date _____

Name of Wine _____   Vintage _____

Varietal _____   Bottle Price _____

Aroma Notes:	Tasting Notes:

Hint: Use Wine Characteristics Chart

Color:

Maroon

Garnet

Ruby

Fuchsia

Salmon

Peach

Amber

Gold

Straw

Overall Impression:

Pairing Ideas:

Fill wine glasses for Deliciousness Rating:

Winery _____ Region_____

Winery Tour Experience

Appointment / reservation required? Y / N

Winery recommended by: ....

Winery Story: ....

....

....

....

....

....

Key information learned: ....

....

....

....

Tasting Room Experience

Appointment / reservation required? Y / N

Cost of tasting: .... Name of Pourer ....

Description of tasting room: ....

....

....

....

....

Recommendations for future visits: ....

....

....

Tasting Notes

Winery _____   Date _____

Name of Wine _____   Vintage _____

Varietal _____   Bottle Price _____

Aroma Notes:	Tasting Notes:

Hint: Use Wine Characteristics Chart

Color:

Maroon

Garnet

Ruby

Fuchsia

Salmon

Peach

Amber

Gold

Straw

Overall Impression:

Pairing Ideas:

Fill wine glasses for Deliciousness Rating:

Tasting Notes

Winery _____   Date _____
Name of Wine _____   Vintage _____
Varietal _____   Bottle Price _____

Aroma Notes:	Tasting Notes:

Hint: Use Wine Characteristics Chart

Color:

Maroon

Garnet

Ruby

Fuchsia

Salmon

Peach

Amber

Gold

Straw

Overall Impression:

Pairing Ideas:

Fill wine glasses for
Deliciousness
Rating:

Tasting Notes

Winery _____   Date _____
Name of Wine _____   Vintage _____
Varietal _____   Bottle Price _____

Aroma Notes:	Tasting Notes:

Hint: Use Wine Characteristics Chart

Color:

	Maroon
	Garnet
	Ruby
	Fuchsia
	Salmon
	Peach
	Amber
	Gold
	Straw

Overall Impression:

Pairing Ideas:

Fill wine glasses for Deliciousness Rating:

Tasting Notes

Winery _____   Date _____
Name of Wine _____   Vintage _____
Varietal _____   Bottle Price _____

Aroma Notes:	Tasting Notes:

Hint: Use Wine Characteristics Chart

Color:

- Maroon
- Garnet
- Ruby
- Fuchsia
- Salmon
- Peach
- Amber
- Gold
- Straw

Overall Impression:

Pairing Ideas:

Fill wine glasses for Deliciousness Rating:

Tasting Notes

Winery _____   Date _____

Name of Wine _____   Vintage _____

Varietal _____   Bottle Price _____

Aroma Notes:	Tasting Notes:

Hint: Use Wine Characteristics Chart

Color:

- Maroon
- Garnet
- Ruby
- Fuchsia
- Salmon
- Peach
- Amber
- Gold
- Straw

Overall Impression:

Pairing Ideas:

Fill wine glasses for
Deliciousness
Rating:

Tasting Notes

Winery _____   Date _____
Name of Wine _____   Vintage _____
Varietal _____   Bottle Price _____

Aroma Notes:	Tasting Notes:

Hint: Use Wine Characteristics Chart

Color:

Maroon

Garnet

Ruby

Fuchsia

Salmon

Peach

Amber

Gold

Straw

Overall Impression:

Pairing Ideas:

Fill wine glasses for
Deliciousness
Rating:

Tasting Notes

Winery _____   Date _____
Name of Wine _____   Vintage _____
Varietal _____   Bottle Price _____

Aroma Notes:	Tasting Notes:

Hint: Use Wine Characteristics Chart

Color:

- Maroon
- Garnet
- Ruby
- Fuchsia
- Salmon
- Peach
- Amber
- Gold
- Straw

Overall Impression:

Pairing Ideas:

Fill wine glasses for Deliciousness Rating:

Tasting Notes

Winery _____   Date _____
Name of Wine _____   Vintage _____
Varietal _____   Bottle Price _____

Aroma Notes:	Tasting Notes:

Hint: Use Wine Characteristics Chart

Color:

Maroon

Garnet

Ruby

Fuchsia

Salmon

Peach

Amber

Gold

Straw

Overall Impression:

Pairing Ideas:

Fill wine glasses for
Deliciousness
Rating:

Winery _____ Region_____

Winery Tour Experience

Appointment / reservation required? Y / N

Winery recommended by: ....…..........................

Winery Story: ....…....

....…..................……...

....……...…...

....….........

....…..................

....…..................

Key information learned: ....…..........................….......

....….........

....…..................

....…..................……...

Tasting Room Experience

Appointment / reservation required? Y / N

Cost of tasting: ...…............. Name of Pourer ....…..….........

Description of tasting room: ....…................................…....

....…..........

....….........

....…...

....…..................

Recommendations for future visits: ..…......................….…........

....…..................

....…..................……...

Tasting Notes

Winery _____   Date _____

Name of Wine _____   Vintage _____

Varietal _____   Bottle Price _____

Aroma Notes:	Tasting Notes:

Hint: Use Wine Characteristics Chart

Color:

	Maroon
	Garnet
	Ruby
	Fuchsia
	Salmon
	Peach
	Amber
	Gold
	Straw

Overall Impression:

Pairing Ideas:

Fill wine glasses for
Deliciousness
Rating:

Tasting Notes

Winery _____   Date _____

Name of Wine _____   Vintage _____

Varietal _____   Bottle Price _____

Aroma Notes:	Tasting Notes:

Hint: Use Wine Characteristics Chart

Color:

- Maroon
- Garnet
- Ruby
- Fuchsia
- Salmon
- Peach
- Amber
- Gold
- Straw

Overall Impression:

Pairing Ideas:

Fill wine glasses for
Deliciousness
Rating:

Tasting Notes

Winery _____   Date _____
Name of Wine _____   Vintage _____
Varietal _____   Bottle Price _____

Aroma Notes: Tasting Notes:

Hint: Use Wine Characteristics Chart

Color: Overall Impression:

☐ Maroon

☐ Garnet

☐ Ruby

☐ Fuchsia

☐ Salmon

☐ Peach   Pairing Ideas:

☐ Amber

☐ Gold

☐ Straw

Fill wine glasses for
Deliciousness
Rating: 🍷 🍷 🍷 🍷 🍷

Tasting Notes

Winery _____   Date _____

Name of Wine _____   Vintage _____

Varietal _____   Bottle Price _____

Aroma Notes:	Tasting Notes:

Hint: Use Wine Characteristics Chart

Color:

- Maroon
- Garnet
- Ruby
- Fuchsia
- Salmon
- Peach
- Amber
- Gold
- Straw

Overall Impression:

Pairing Ideas:

Fill wine glasses for Deliciousness Rating:

Tasting Notes

Winery _____   Date _____
Name of Wine _____   Vintage _____
Varietal _____   Bottle Price _____

Aroma Notes:	Tasting Notes:

Hint: Use Wine Characteristics Chart

Color:

Maroon

Garnet

Ruby

Fuchsia

Salmon

Peach

Amber

Gold

Straw

Overall Impression:

Pairing Ideas:

Fill wine glasses for
Deliciousness
Rating:

Tasting Notes

Winery _____   Date _____
Name of Wine _____   Vintage _____
Varietal _____   Bottle Price _____

Aroma Notes:	Tasting Notes:

Hint: Use Wine Characteristics Chart

Color:

Maroon

Garnet

Ruby

Fuchsia

Salmon

Peach

Amber

Gold

Straw

Overall Impression:

Pairing Ideas:

Fill wine glasses for
Deliciousness
Rating:

Tasting Notes

Winery _____   Date _____

Name of Wine _____   Vintage _____

Varietal _____   Bottle Price _____

Aroma Notes:	Tasting Notes:

Hint: Use Wine Characteristics Chart

Color:

	Maroon
	Garnet
	Ruby
	Fuchsia
	Salmon
	Peach
	Amber
	Gold
	Straw

Overall Impression:

Pairing Ideas:

Fill wine glasses for Deliciousness Rating:

Tasting Notes

Winery _____   Date _____

Name of Wine _____   Vintage _____

Varietal _____   Bottle Price _____

Aroma Notes:	Tasting Notes:

Hint: Use Wine Characteristics Chart

Color:

Maroon

Garnet

Ruby

Fuchsia

Salmon

Peach

Amber

Gold

Straw

Overall Impression:

Pairing Ideas:

Fill wine glasses for
Deliciousness
Rating:

Winery _____ Region_____

Winery Tour Experience

Appointment / reservation required? Y / N

Winery recommended by: ....

Winery Story: ....

....

....

....

....

....

Key information learned: ....

....

....

....

Tasting Room Experience

Appointment / reservation required? Y / N

Cost of tasting: .... Name of Pourer ....

Description of tasting room: ....

....

....

....

....

Recommendations for future visits: ....

....

....

Tasting Notes

Winery _____   Date _____

Name of Wine _____   Vintage _____

Varietal _____   Bottle Price _____

Aroma Notes:	Tasting Notes:

Hint: Use Wine Characteristics Chart

Color:

- Maroon
- Garnet
- Ruby
- Fuchsia
- Salmon
- Peach
- Amber
- Gold
- Straw

Overall Impression:

Pairing Ideas:

Fill wine glasses for Deliciousness Rating:

Tasting Notes

Winery _____   Date _____
Name of Wine _____   Vintage _____
Varietal _____   Bottle Price _____

Aroma Notes:	Tasting Notes:

Hint: Use Wine Characteristics Chart

Color:

	Maroon
	Garnet
	Ruby
	Fuchsia
	Salmon
	Peach
	Amber
	Gold
	Straw

Overall Impression:

Pairing Ideas:

Fill wine glasses for
Deliciousness
Rating:

Tasting Notes

Winery _____   Date _____
Name of Wine _____   Vintage _____
Varietal _____   Bottle Price _____

Aroma Notes:	Tasting Notes:

Hint: Use Wine Characteristics Chart

Color:

- Maroon
- Garnet
- Ruby
- Fuchsia
- Salmon
- Peach
- Amber
- Gold
- Straw

Overall Impression:

Pairing Ideas:

Fill wine glasses for
Deliciousness
Rating:

Tasting Notes

Winery _____   Date _____
Name of Wine _____   Vintage _____
Varietal _____   Bottle Price _____

Aroma Notes:	Tasting Notes:

Hint: Use Wine Characteristics Chart

Color:

	Maroon
	Garnet
	Ruby
	Fuchsia
	Salmon
	Peach
	Amber
	Gold
	Straw

Overall Impression:

Pairing Ideas:

Fill wine glasses for Deliciousness Rating:

Tasting Notes

Winery _____   Date _____
Name of Wine _____   Vintage _____
Varietal _____   Bottle Price _____

Aroma Notes:	Tasting Notes:

Hint: Use Wine Characteristics Chart

Color:

- Maroon
- Garnet
- Ruby
- Fuchsia
- Salmon
- Peach
- Amber
- Gold
- Straw

Overall Impression:

Pairing Ideas:

Fill wine glasses for
Deliciousness
Rating:

Tasting Notes

Winery _____   Date _____
Name of Wine _____   Vintage _____
Varietal _____   Bottle Price _____

Aroma Notes:	Tasting Notes:

Hint: Use Wine Characteristics Chart

Color:

	Maroon
	Garnet
	Ruby
	Fuchsia
	Salmon
	Peach
	Amber
	Gold
	Straw

Overall Impression:

Pairing Ideas:

Fill wine glasses for
Deliciousness
Rating:

Tasting Notes

Winery _____   Date _____
Name of Wine _____   Vintage _____
Varietal _____   Bottle Price _____

Aroma Notes:	Tasting Notes:

Hint: Use Wine Characteristics Chart

Color:

Maroon

Garnet

Ruby

Fuchsia

Salmon

Peach

Amber

Gold

Straw

Overall Impression:

Pairing Ideas:

Fill wine glasses for
Deliciousness
Rating:

Tasting Notes

Winery _____   Date _____
Name of Wine _____   Vintage _____
Varietal _____   Bottle Price _____

Aroma Notes:	Tasting Notes:

Hint: Use Wine Characteristics Chart

Color:

Maroon

Garnet

Ruby

Fuchsia

Salmon

Peach

Amber

Gold

Straw

Overall Impression:

Pairing Ideas:

Fill wine glasses for
Deliciousness
Rating:

Winery _____ Region_____

Winery Tour Experience

Appointment / reservation required? Y / N

Winery recommended by: ....…........................

Winery Story: ....….......

....…..................................

....

....….......

....

....….................................

Key information learned: ....…...........................

....…...........

....…..................

....…..................................

Tasting Room Experience

Appointment / reservation required? Y / N

Cost of tasting: ...…............... Name of Pourer ....…......…........

Description of tasting room: ....…......................................…....

....…...............................

....…..................

....…............................

....…...................

Recommendations for future visits: ..…...................................…........

....…....................

....…............................

Tasting Notes

Winery _____   Date _____

Name of Wine _____   Vintage _____

Varietal _____   Bottle Price _____

Aroma Notes:	Tasting Notes:

Hint: Use Wine Characteristics Chart

Color:

	Maroon
	Garnet
	Ruby
	Fuchsia
	Salmon
	Peach
	Amber
	Gold
	Straw

Overall Impression:

Pairing Ideas:

Fill wine glasses for Deliciousness Rating:

Tasting Notes

Winery _____   Date _____

Name of Wine _____   Vintage _____

Varietal _____   Bottle Price _____

Aroma Notes:	Tasting Notes:

Hint: Use Wine Characteristics Chart

Color:

	Maroon
	Garnet
	Ruby
	Fuchsia
	Salmon
	Peach
	Amber
	Gold
	Straw

Overall Impression:

Pairing Ideas:

Fill wine glasses for Deliciousness Rating:

Tasting Notes

Winery _____   Date _____
Name of Wine _____   Vintage _____
Varietal _____   Bottle Price _____

Aroma Notes:	Tasting Notes:

Hint: Use Wine Characteristics Chart

Color:

- Maroon
- Garnet
- Ruby
- Fuchsia
- Salmon
- Peach
- Amber
- Gold
- Straw

Overall Impression:

Pairing Ideas:

Fill wine glasses for Deliciousness Rating:

Tasting Notes

Winery _____   Date _____

Name of Wine _____   Vintage _____

Varietal _____   Bottle Price _____

Aroma Notes:	Tasting Notes:

Hint: Use Wine Characteristics Chart

Color:

- Maroon
- Garnet
- Ruby
- Fuchsia
- Salmon
- Peach
- Amber
- Gold
- Straw

Overall Impression:

Pairing Ideas:

Fill wine glasses for Deliciousness Rating:

Tasting Notes

Winery _____   Date _____
Name of Wine _____   Vintage _____
Varietal _____   Bottle Price _____

Aroma Notes:	Tasting Notes:

Hint: Use Wine Characteristics Chart

Color:

Maroon

Garnet

Ruby

Fuchsia

Salmon

Peach

Amber

Gold

Straw

Overall Impression:

Pairing Ideas:

Fill wine glasses for
Deliciousness
Rating:

Tasting Notes

Winery _____   Date _____
Name of Wine _____   Vintage _____
Varietal _____   Bottle Price _____

Aroma Notes:	Tasting Notes:

Hint: Use Wine Characteristics Chart

Color:

Overall Impression:

- Maroon
- Garnet
- Ruby
- Fuchsia
- Salmon
- Peach
- Amber
- Gold
- Straw

Pairing Ideas:

Fill wine glasses for
Deliciousness
Rating:

Tasting Notes

Winery _____   Date _____
Name of Wine _____   Vintage _____
Varietal _____   Bottle Price _____

Aroma Notes:	Tasting Notes:

Hint: Use Wine Characteristics Chart

Color:

Maroon

Garnet

Ruby

Fuchsia

Salmon

Peach

Amber

Gold

Straw

Overall Impression:

Pairing Ideas:

Fill wine glasses for
Deliciousness
Rating:

Tasting Notes

Winery _____   Date _____
Name of Wine _____   Vintage _____
Varietal _____   Bottle Price _____

Aroma Notes:	Tasting Notes:

Hint: Use Wine Characteristics Chart

Color:

Maroon

Garnet

Ruby

Fuchsia

Salmon

Peach

Amber

Gold

Straw

Overall Impression:

Pairing Ideas:

Fill wine glasses for
Deliciousness
Rating:

Winery _____ Region_____

Winery Tour Experience

Appointment / reservation required? Y / N

Winery recommended by: ....…........................…..

Winery Story: ....…........................…...

....…........…................…...

....…........…................…...

....…........…................…...

....…........…................…...

....…........…................…...

Key information learned: ....…...............................…....

....…........…................…...

....…........…................…...

....…........…................…...

Tasting Room Experience

Appointment / reservation required? Y / N

Cost of tasting: ...…............... Name of Pourer ....…......

Description of tasting room: ....…................….

....…........…................…...

....…........…................…...

....…........…................…...

....…........…................…...

Recommendations for future visits: ..…...............................….........

....…........…................…...

....…........…................…...

Tasting Notes

Winery _____   Date _____
Name of Wine _____   Vintage _____
Varietal _____   Bottle Price _____

Aroma Notes:	Tasting Notes:

Hint: Use Wine Characteristics Chart

Color:

Maroon

Garnet

Ruby

Fuchsia

Salmon

Peach

Amber

Gold

Straw

Overall Impression:

Pairing Ideas:

Fill wine glasses for
Deliciousness
Rating:

Tasting Notes

Winery _____   Date _____
Name of Wine _____   Vintage _____
Varietal _____   Bottle Price _____

Aroma Notes:	Tasting Notes:

Hint: Use Wine Characteristics Chart

Color:

- Maroon
- Garnet
- Ruby
- Fuchsia
- Salmon
- Peach
- Amber
- Gold
- Straw

Overall Impression:

Pairing Ideas:

Fill wine glasses for Deliciousness Rating:

Tasting Notes

Winery _____ Date _____
Name of Wine _____ Vintage _____
Varietal _____ Bottle Price _____

Aroma Notes:	Tasting Notes:

Hint: Use Wine Characteristics Chart

Color:

Maroon

Garnet

Ruby

Fuchsia

Salmon

Peach

Amber

Gold

Straw

Overall Impression:

Pairing Ideas:

Fill wine glasses for
Deliciousness
Rating:

Tasting Notes

Winery _____   Date _____
Name of Wine _____   Vintage _____
Varietal _____   Bottle Price _____

Aroma Notes:	Tasting Notes:

Hint: Use Wine Characteristics Chart

Color:

- Maroon
- Garnet
- Ruby
- Fuchsia
- Salmon
- Peach
- Amber
- Gold
- Straw

Overall Impression:

Pairing Ideas:

Fill wine glasses for
Deliciousness
Rating:

Tasting Notes

Winery _____   Date _____
Name of Wine _____   Vintage _____
Varietal _____   Bottle Price _____

Aroma Notes:	Tasting Notes:

Hint: Use Wine Characteristics Chart

Color:

- Maroon
- Garnet
- Ruby
- Fuchsia
- Salmon
- Peach
- Amber
- Gold
- Straw

Overall Impression:

Pairing Ideas:

Fill wine glasses for
Deliciousness
Rating:

Tasting Notes

Winery _____   Date _____

Name of Wine _____   Vintage _____

Varietal _____   Bottle Price _____

Aroma Notes:	Tasting Notes:

Hint: Use Wine Characteristics Chart

Color:

Maroon

Garnet

Ruby

Fuchsia

Salmon

Peach

Amber

Gold

Straw

Overall Impression:

Pairing Ideas:

Fill wine glasses for
Deliciousness
Rating:

Tasting Notes

Winery _____   Date _____
Name of Wine _____   Vintage _____
Varietal _____   Bottle Price _____

Aroma Notes:	Tasting Notes:

Hint: Use Wine Characteristics Chart

Color:

Maroon

Garnet

Ruby

Fuchsia

Salmon

Peach

Amber

Gold

Straw

Overall Impression:

Pairing Ideas:

Fill wine glasses for
Deliciousness
Rating:

Tasting Notes

Winery _____   Date _____

Name of Wine _____   Vintage _____

Varietal _____   Bottle Price _____

Aroma Notes:	Tasting Notes:

Hint: Use Wine Characteristics Chart

Color:

Maroon

Garnet

Ruby

Fuchsia

Salmon

Peach

Amber

Gold

Straw

Overall Impression:

Pairing Ideas:

Fill wine glasses for
Deliciousness
Rating:

Winery _____ Region_____

Winery Tour Experience

Appointment / reservation required? Y / N

Winery recommended by: ....…..................................

Winery Story: ....

....…...............….............

....……...........

....…..............................

....…..............................

....…..............................

Key information learned: ....…......................…..........

....….............

....…..............................

....…..…....................….........

Tasting Room Experience

Appointment / reservation required? Y / N

Cost of tasting: ...…............... Name of Pourer ....…...…..........

Description of tasting room: ....….....…...….......................…....

....….................….............

....…..........................…......

....…...............................

....…..............................

Recommendations for future visits: ....….....……...…..........

....…..............................

....…...............................

Tasting Notes

Winery _____   Date _____

Name of Wine _____   Vintage _____

Varietal _____   Bottle Price _____

Aroma Notes:	Tasting Notes:

Hint: Use Wine Characteristics Chart

Color:

Maroon

Garnet

Ruby

Fuchsia

Salmon

Peach

Amber

Gold

Straw

Overall Impression:

Pairing Ideas:

Fill wine glasses for
Deliciousness
Rating:

Tasting Notes

Winery _____   Date _____
Name of Wine _____   Vintage _____
Varietal _____   Bottle Price _____

Aroma Notes:	Tasting Notes:

Hint: Use Wine Characteristics Chart

Color:

Maroon

Garnet

Ruby

Fuchsia

Salmon

Peach

Amber

Gold

Straw

Overall Impression:

Pairing Ideas:

Fill wine glasses for
Deliciousness
Rating:

Tasting Notes

Winery _____   Date _____
Name of Wine _____   Vintage _____
Varietal _____   Bottle Price _____

Aroma Notes:	Tasting Notes:

Hint: Use Wine Characteristics Chart

Color:

Overall Impression:

Maroon

Garnet

Ruby

Fuchsia

Salmon

Peach

Amber

Gold

Straw

Pairing Ideas:

Fill wine glasses for
Deliciousness
Rating:

Tasting Notes

Winery _____   Date _____

Name of Wine _____   Vintage _____

Varietal _____   Bottle Price _____

Aroma Notes:	Tasting Notes:

Hint: Use Wine Characteristics Chart

Color:

	Maroon
	Garnet
	Ruby
	Fuchsia
	Salmon
	Peach
	Amber
	Gold
	Straw

Overall Impression:

Pairing Ideas:

Fill wine glasses for Deliciousness Rating:

Tasting Notes

Winery _____   Date _____
Name of Wine _____   Vintage _____
Varietal _____   Bottle Price _____

Aroma Notes:	Tasting Notes:

Hint: Use Wine Characteristics Chart

Color:

Maroon

Garnet

Ruby

Fuchsia

Salmon

Peach

Amber

Gold

Straw

Overall Impression:

Pairing Ideas:

Fill wine glasses for
Deliciousness
Rating:

Tasting Notes

Winery _____   Date _____

Name of Wine _____   Vintage _____

Varietal _____   Bottle Price _____

Aroma Notes:	Tasting Notes:

Hint: Use Wine Characteristics Chart

Color:

- Maroon
- Garnet
- Ruby
- Fuchsia
- Salmon
- Peach
- Amber
- Gold
- Straw

Overall Impression:

Pairing Ideas:

Fill wine glasses for Deliciousness Rating:

Tasting Notes

Winery _____   Date _____

Name of Wine _____   Vintage _____

Varietal _____   Bottle Price _____

Aroma Notes:	Tasting Notes:

Hint: Use Wine Characteristics Chart

Color:

Maroon

Garnet

Ruby

Fuchsia

Salmon

Peach

Amber

Gold

Straw

Overall Impression:

Pairing Ideas:

Fill wine glasses for Deliciousness Rating:

Tasting Notes

Winery _____   Date _____
Name of Wine _____   Vintage _____
Varietal _____   Bottle Price _____

Aroma Notes:	Tasting Notes:

Hint: Use Wine Characteristics Chart

Color:

- Maroon
- Garnet
- Ruby
- Fuchsia
- Salmon
- Peach
- Amber
- Gold
- Straw

Overall Impression:

Pairing Ideas:

Fill wine glasses for
Deliciousness
Rating:

138

Winery _____ *Region*_____

Winery Tour Experience

Appointment / reservation required? Y / N

Winery recommended by: ....

Winery Story: ....

....

....

....

....

....

Key information learned: ....

....

....

....

Tasting Room Experience

Appointment / reservation required? Y / N

Cost of tasting: .... Name of Pourer ....

Description of tasting room: ....

....

....

....

....

Recommendations for future visits: ....

....

....

Tasting Notes

Winery _____   Date _____
Name of Wine _____   Vintage _____
Varietal _____   Bottle Price _____

Aroma Notes:	Tasting Notes:

Hint: Use Wine Characteristics Chart

Color:

- Maroon
- Garnet
- Ruby
- Fuchsia
- Salmon
- Peach
- Amber
- Gold
- Straw

Overall Impression:

Pairing Ideas:

Fill wine glasses for
Deliciousness
Rating:

Tasting Notes

Winery _____   Date _____

Name of Wine _____   Vintage _____

Varietal _____   Bottle Price _____

Aroma Notes:	Tasting Notes:

Hint: Use Wine Characteristics Chart

Color:

Maroon

Garnet

Ruby

Fuchsia

Salmon

Peach

Amber

Gold

Straw

Overall Impression:

Pairing Ideas:

Fill wine glasses for Deliciousness Rating:

Tasting Notes

Winery _____   Date _____

Name of Wine _____   Vintage _____

Varietal _____   Bottle Price _____

Aroma Notes:	Tasting Notes:

Hint: Use Wine Characteristics Chart

Color:

	Maroon
	Garnet
	Ruby
	Fuchsia
	Salmon
	Peach
	Amber
	Gold
	Straw

Overall Impression:

Pairing Ideas:

Fill wine glasses for
Deliciousness
Rating:

Tasting Notes

Winery _____   Date _____
Name of Wine _____   Vintage _____
Varietal _____   Bottle Price _____

Aroma Notes:

Tasting Notes:

Hint: Use Wine Characteristics Chart

Color:

Maroon

Garnet

Ruby

Fuchsia

Salmon

Peach

Amber

Gold

Straw

Overall Impression:

Pairing Ideas:

Fill wine glasses for
Deliciousness
Rating:

Tasting Notes

Winery _____   Date _____

Name of Wine _____   Vintage _____

Varietal _____   Bottle Price _____

Aroma Notes:	Tasting Notes:

Hint: Use Wine Characteristics Chart

Color:

- Maroon
- Garnet
- Ruby
- Fuchsia
- Salmon
- Peach
- Amber
- Gold
- Straw

Overall Impression:

Pairing Ideas:

Fill wine glasses for Deliciousness Rating:

Tasting Notes

Winery _____   Date _____

Name of Wine _____   Vintage _____

Varietal _____   Bottle Price _____

Aroma Notes:	Tasting Notes:

Hint: Use Wine Characteristics Chart

Color:

- Maroon
- Garnet
- Ruby
- Fuchsia
- Salmon
- Peach
- Amber
- Gold
- Straw

Overall Impression:

Pairing Ideas:

Fill wine glasses for Deliciousness Rating:

Tasting Notes

Winery _____   Date _____
Name of Wine _____   Vintage _____
Varietal _____   Bottle Price _____

Aroma Notes:	Tasting Notes:

Hint: Use Wine Characteristics Chart

Color:

Maroon

Garnet

Ruby

Fuchsia

Salmon

Peach

Amber

Gold

Straw

Overall Impression:

Pairing Ideas:

Fill wine glasses for
Deliciousness
Rating:

Tasting Notes

Winery _____   Date _____

Name of Wine _____   Vintage _____

Varietal _____   Bottle Price _____

Aroma Notes:	Tasting Notes:

Hint: Use Wine Characteristics Chart

Color:

Maroon

Garnet

Ruby

Fuchsia

Salmon

Peach

Amber

Gold

Straw

Overall Impression:

Pairing Ideas:

Fill wine glasses for
Deliciousness
Rating:

Winery _____ Region_____

Winery Tour Experience

Appointment / reservation required? Y / N

Winery recommended by: ....

Winery Story: ....

....

....

....

....

....

Key information learned: ....

....

....

....

Tasting Room Experience

Appointment / reservation required? Y / N

Cost of tasting: .... Name of Pourer ....

Description of tasting room: ....

....

....

....

....

Recommendations for future visits: ....

....

....

Tasting Notes

Winery _____   Date _____
Name of Wine _____   Vintage _____
Varietal _____   Bottle Price _____

Aroma Notes:	Tasting Notes:

Hint: Use Wine Characteristics Chart

Color:

Overall Impression:

- Maroon
- Garnet
- Ruby
- Fuchsia
- Salmon
- Peach
- Amber
- Gold
- Straw

Pairing Ideas:

Fill wine glasses for
Deliciousness
Rating:

Tasting Notes

Winery _____   Date _____
Name of Wine _____   Vintage _____
Varietal _____   Bottle Price _____

Aroma Notes:	Tasting Notes:

Hint: Use Wine Characteristics Chart

Color:

Maroon

Garnet

Ruby

Fuchsia

Salmon

Peach

Amber

Gold

Straw

Overall Impression:

Pairing Ideas:

Fill wine glasses for
Deliciousness
Rating:

Tasting Notes

Winery _____   Date _____

Name of Wine _____   Vintage _____

Varietal _____   Bottle Price _____

Aroma Notes:	Tasting Notes:

Hint: Use Wine Characteristics Chart

Color:

☐	Maroon
☐	Garnet
☐	Ruby
☐	Fuchsia
☐	Salmon
☐	Peach
☐	Amber
☐	Gold
☐	Straw

Overall Impression:

Pairing Ideas:

Fill wine glasses for
Deliciousness
Rating:

Tasting Notes

Winery _____   Date _____

Name of Wine _____   Vintage _____

Varietal _____   Bottle Price _____

Aroma Notes:	Tasting Notes:

Hint: Use Wine Characteristics Chart

Color:

- Maroon
- Garnet
- Ruby
- Fuchsia
- Salmon
- Peach
- Amber
- Gold
- Straw

Overall Impression:

Pairing Ideas:

Fill wine glasses for
Deliciousness
Rating:

Tasting Notes

Winery _____   Date _____
Name of Wine _____   Vintage _____
Varietal _____   Bottle Price _____

Aroma Notes:	Tasting Notes:

Hint: Use Wine Characteristics Chart

Color:

Maroon

Garnet

Ruby

Fuchsia

Salmon

Peach

Amber

Gold

Straw

Overall Impression:

Pairing Ideas:

Fill wine glasses for
Deliciousness
Rating:

Tasting Notes

Winery _____   Date _____
Name of Wine _____   Vintage _____
Varietal _____   Bottle Price _____

Aroma Notes:	Tasting Notes:

Hint: Use Wine Characteristics Chart

Color:

	Maroon
	Garnet
	Ruby
	Fuchsia
	Salmon
	Peach
	Amber
	Gold
	Straw

Overall Impression:

Pairing Ideas:

Fill wine glasses for
Deliciousness
Rating:

Tasting Notes

Winery _____   Date _____

Name of Wine _____   Vintage _____

Varietal _____   Bottle Price _____

Aroma Notes:	Tasting Notes:

Hint: Use Wine Characteristics Chart

Color:

	Maroon
	Garnet
	Ruby
	Fuchsia
	Salmon
	Peach
	Amber
	Gold
	Straw

Overall Impression:

Pairing Ideas:

Fill wine glasses for Deliciousness Rating:

Tasting Notes

Winery _____   Date _____

Name of Wine _____   Vintage _____

Varietal _____   Bottle Price _____

Aroma Notes:	Tasting Notes:

Hint: Use Wine Characteristics Chart

Color:

- Maroon
- Garnet
- Ruby
- Fuchsia
- Salmon
- Peach
- Amber
- Gold
- Straw

Overall Impression:

Pairing Ideas:

Fill wine glasses for Deliciousness Rating:

Winery _____ Region_____

Winery Tour Experience

Appointment / reservation required? Y / N

Winery recommended by: ....

Winery Story: ....

....

....

....

....

....

Key information learned: ....

....

....

....

Tasting Room Experience

Appointment / reservation required? Y / N

Cost of tasting: .... Name of Pourer ....

Description of tasting room: ....

....

....

....

....

Recommendations for future visits: ....

....

....

Tasting Notes

Winery _____   Date _____

Name of Wine _____   Vintage _____

Varietal _____   Bottle Price _____

Aroma Notes:	Tasting Notes:

Hint: Use Wine Characteristics Chart

Color:

Maroon

Garnet

Ruby

Fuchsia

Salmon

Peach

Amber

Gold

Straw

Overall Impression:

Pairing Ideas:

Fill wine glasses for
Deliciousness
Rating:

Tasting Notes

Winery _____   Date _____

Name of Wine _____   Vintage _____

Varietal _____   Bottle Price _____

Aroma Notes:	Tasting Notes:

Hint: Use Wine Characteristics Chart

Color:

	Maroon
	Garnet
	Ruby
	Fuchsia
	Salmon
	Peach
	Amber
	Gold
	Straw

Overall Impression:

Pairing Ideas:

Fill wine glasses for
Deliciousness
Rating:

Tasting Notes

Winery _____   Date _____

Name of Wine _____   Vintage _____

Varietal _____   Bottle Price _____

Aroma Notes:	Tasting Notes:

Hint: Use Wine Characteristics Chart

Color:

	Maroon
	Garnet
	Ruby
	Fuchsia
	Salmon
	Peach
	Amber
	Gold
	Straw

Overall Impression:

Pairing Ideas:

Fill wine glasses for
Deliciousness
Rating:

Tasting Notes

Winery _____   Date _____
Name of Wine _____   Vintage _____
Varietal _____   Bottle Price _____

Aroma Notes:	Tasting Notes:

Hint: Use Wine Characteristics Chart

Color:

Overall Impression:

- Maroon
- Garnet
- Ruby
- Fuchsia
- Salmon
- Peach
- Amber
- Gold
- Straw

Pairing Ideas:

Fill wine glasses for
Deliciousness
Rating:

Tasting Notes

Winery _____   Date _____

Name of Wine _____   Vintage _____

Varietal _____   Bottle Price _____

Aroma Notes:	Tasting Notes:

Hint: Use Wine Characteristics Chart

Color:

Maroon

Garnet

Ruby

Fuchsia

Salmon

Peach

Amber

Gold

Straw

Overall Impression:

Pairing Ideas:

Fill wine glasses for Deliciousness Rating:

Tasting Notes

Winery _____   Date _____
Name of Wine _____   Vintage _____
Varietal _____   Bottle Price _____

Aroma Notes:	Tasting Notes:

Hint: Use Wine Characteristics Chart

Color:

- Maroon
- Garnet
- Ruby
- Fuchsia
- Salmon
- Peach
- Amber
- Gold
- Straw

Overall Impression:

Pairing Ideas:

Fill wine glasses for
Deliciousness
Rating:

Tasting Notes

Winery _____   Date _____

Name of Wine _____   Vintage _____

Varietal _____   Bottle Price _____

Aroma Notes:	Tasting Notes:

Hint: Use Wine Characteristics Chart

Color:

	Maroon
	Garnet
	Ruby
	Fuchsia
	Salmon
	Peach
	Amber
	Gold
	Straw

Overall Impression:

Pairing Ideas:

Fill wine glasses for
Deliciousness
Rating:

Tasting Notes

Winery _____   Date _____

Name of Wine _____   Vintage _____

Varietal _____   Bottle Price _____

Aroma Notes:	Tasting Notes:

Hint: Use Wine Characteristics Chart

Color:

Maroon

Garnet

Ruby

Fuchsia

Salmon

Peach

Amber

Gold

Straw

Overall Impression:

Pairing Ideas:

Fill wine glasses for
Deliciousness
Rating:

Winery _____ Region_____

Winery Tour Experience

Appointment / reservation required? Y / N

Winery recommended by: ....…................................

Winery Story: ....

....

....

....

....

....

Key information learned: ....…...............................…....

....

....

....

Tasting Room Experience

Appointment / reservation required? Y / N

Cost of tasting: ...…............... Name of Pourer ....…............…..

Description of tasting room: ....…........................…...

....

....

....

....

Recommendations for future visits: .....…...............................…........

....

....

Tasting Notes

Winery _____   Date _____
Name of Wine _____   Vintage _____
Varietal _____   Bottle Price _____

Aroma Notes:	Tasting Notes:

Hint: Use Wine Characteristics Chart

Color:

- Maroon
- Garnet
- Ruby
- Fuchsia
- Salmon
- Peach
- Amber
- Gold
- Straw

Overall Impression:

Pairing Ideas:

Fill wine glasses for
Deliciousness
Rating:

Tasting Notes

Winery _____   Date _____
Name of Wine _____   Vintage _____
Varietal _____   Bottle Price _____

Aroma Notes:	Tasting Notes:

Hint: Use Wine Characteristics Chart

Color:

Maroon

Garnet

Ruby

Fuchsia

Salmon

Peach

Amber

Gold

Straw

Overall Impression:

Pairing Ideas:

Fill wine glasses for
Deliciousness
Rating:

Tasting Notes

Winery _____   Date _____

Name of Wine _____   Vintage _____

Varietal _____   Bottle Price _____

Aroma Notes:	Tasting Notes:

Hint: Use Wine Characteristics Chart

Color:

- Maroon
- Garnet
- Ruby
- Fuchsia
- Salmon
- Peach
- Amber
- Gold
- Straw

Overall Impression:

Pairing Ideas:

Fill wine glasses for Deliciousness Rating:

Tasting Notes

Winery _____   Date _____
Name of Wine _____   Vintage _____
Varietal _____   Bottle Price _____

Aroma Notes:	Tasting Notes:

Hint: Use Wine Characteristics Chart

Color:

Maroon

Garnet

Ruby

Fuchsia

Salmon

Peach

Amber

Gold

Straw

Overall Impression:

Pairing Ideas:

Fill wine glasses for
Deliciousness
Rating:

Tasting Notes

Winery _____   Date _____

Name of Wine _____   Vintage _____

Varietal _____   Bottle Price _____

Aroma Notes:	Tasting Notes:

Hint: Use Wine Characteristics Chart

Color:

- Maroon
- Garnet
- Ruby
- Fuchsia
- Salmon
- Peach
- Amber
- Gold
- Straw

Overall Impression:

Pairing Ideas:

Fill wine glasses for Deliciousness Rating:

Tasting Notes

Winery _____   Date _____

Name of Wine _____   Vintage _____

Varietal _____   Bottle Price _____

Aroma Notes:	Tasting Notes:

Hint: Use Wine Characteristics Chart

Color:

- Maroon
- Garnet
- Ruby
- Fuchsia
- Salmon
- Peach
- Amber
- Gold
- Straw

Overall Impression:

Pairing Ideas:

Fill wine glasses for
Deliciousness
Rating:

Tasting Notes

Winery _____   Date _____
Name of Wine _____   Vintage _____
Varietal _____   Bottle Price _____

Aroma Notes:	Tasting Notes:

Hint: Use Wine Characteristics Chart

Color:

- Maroon
- Garnet
- Ruby
- Fuchsia
- Salmon
- Peach
- Amber
- Gold
- Straw

Overall Impression:

Pairing Ideas:

Fill wine glasses for
Deliciousness
Rating:

Tasting Notes

Winery _____   Date _____
Name of Wine _____   Vintage _____
Varietal _____   Bottle Price _____

Aroma Notes:	Tasting Notes:

Hint: Use Wine Characteristics Chart

Color:

Maroon

Garnet

Ruby

Fuchsia

Salmon

Peach

Amber

Gold

Straw

Overall Impression:

Pairing Ideas:

Fill wine glasses for Deliciousness Rating:

Winery _____ Region_____

Winery Tour Experience

Appointment / reservation required? Y / N

Winery recommended by: ....…...........................

Winery Story: ....…...................................

....…...…...

....…......

....…......

....…......

....…......

Key information learned: ....…......

....…......

....…......

....…......

Tasting Room Experience

Appointment / reservation required? Y / N

Cost of tasting: ...….............. Name of Pourer ....…....….......

Description of tasting room: ....…....................

....…......

....…......

....…......

....…......

Recommendations for future visits: .....…...........................…......

....…......

....…......

Tasting Notes

Winery _____   Date _____

Name of Wine _____   Vintage _____

Varietal _____   Bottle Price _____

Aroma Notes:	Tasting Notes:

Hint: Use Wine Characteristics Chart

Color:

Maroon

Garnet

Ruby

Fuchsia

Salmon

Peach

Amber

Gold

Straw

Overall Impression:

Pairing Ideas:

Fill wine glasses for
Deliciousness
Rating:

Tasting Notes

Winery _____   Date _____

Name of Wine _____   Vintage _____

Varietal _____   Bottle Price _____

Aroma Notes:	Tasting Notes:

Hint: Use Wine Characteristics Chart

Color:

Maroon

Garnet

Ruby

Fuchsia

Salmon

Peach

Amber

Gold

Straw

Overall Impression:

Pairing Ideas:

Fill wine glasses for
Deliciousness
Rating:

Tasting Notes

Winery _____   Date _____
Name of Wine _____   Vintage _____
Varietal _____   Bottle Price _____

Aroma Notes:

Tasting Notes:

Hint: Use Wine Characteristics Chart

Color:

Maroon

Garnet

Ruby

Fuchsia

Salmon

Peach

Amber

Gold

Straw

Overall Impression:

Pairing Ideas:

Fill wine glasses for
Deliciousness
Rating:

Tasting Notes

Winery _____   Date _____
Name of Wine _____   Vintage _____
Varietal _____   Bottle Price _____

Aroma Notes:	Tasting Notes:

Hint: Use Wine Characteristics Chart

Color:

- Maroon
- Garnet
- Ruby
- Fuchsia
- Salmon
- Peach
- Amber
- Gold
- Straw

Overall Impression:

Pairing Ideas:

Fill wine glasses for
Deliciousness
Rating:

Tasting Notes

Winery _____   Date _____

Name of Wine _____   Vintage _____

Varietal _____   Bottle Price _____

Aroma Notes:	Tasting Notes:

Hint: Use Wine Characteristics Chart

Color:

Overall Impression:

- Maroon
- Garnet
- Ruby
- Fuchsia
- Salmon
- Peach
- Amber
- Gold
- Straw

Pairing Ideas:

Fill wine glasses for Deliciousness Rating:

Tasting Notes

Winery _____   Date _____

Name of Wine _____   Vintage _____

Varietal _____   Bottle Price _____

Aroma Notes:	Tasting Notes:

Hint: Use Wine Characteristics Chart

Color:

- Maroon
- Garnet
- Ruby
- Fuchsia
- Salmon
- Peach
- Amber
- Gold
- Straw

Overall Impression:

Pairing Ideas:

Fill wine glasses for
Deliciousness
Rating:

181

Tasting Notes

Winery _____   Date _____
Name of Wine _____   Vintage _____
Varietal _____   Bottle Price _____

Aroma Notes:	Tasting Notes:

Hint: Use Wine Characteristics Chart

Color:

Maroon

Garnet

Ruby

Fuchsia

Salmon

Peach

Amber

Gold

Straw

Overall Impression:

Pairing Ideas:

Fill wine glasses for
Deliciousness
Rating:

Tasting Notes

Winery _____   Date _____
Name of Wine _____   Vintage _____
Varietal _____   Bottle Price _____

Aroma Notes:	Tasting Notes:

Hint: Use Wine Characteristics Chart

Color:

Overall Impression:

- Maroon
- Garnet
- Ruby
- Fuchsia
- Salmon
- Peach
- Amber
- Gold
- Straw

Pairing Ideas:

Fill wine glasses for
Deliciousness
Rating:

Additional
Tasting Notes

Tasting Notes

Winery _____ Date _____

Name of Wine _____ Vintage _____

Varietal _____ Bottle Price _____

Aroma Notes:	Tasting Notes:

Hint: Use Wine Characteristics Chart

Color:

	Maroon
	Garnet
	Ruby
	Fuchsia
	Salmon
	Peach
	Amber
	Gold
	Straw

Overall Impression:

Pairing Ideas:

Fill wine glasses for Deliciousness Rating:

Tasting Notes

Winery _____   Date _____
Name of Wine _____   Vintage _____
Varietal _____   Bottle Price _____

Aroma Notes:	Tasting Notes:

Hint: Use Wine Characteristics Chart

Color:

- Maroon
- Garnet
- Ruby
- Fuchsia
- Salmon
- Peach
- Amber
- Gold
- Straw

Overall Impression:

Pairing Ideas:

Fill wine glasses for Deliciousness Rating:

Tasting Notes

Winery _____   Date _____

Name of Wine _____   Vintage _____

Varietal _____   Bottle Price _____

Aroma Notes:	Tasting Notes:

Hint: Use Wine Characteristics Chart

Color:

	Maroon
	Garnet
	Ruby
	Fuchsia
	Salmon
	Peach
	Amber
	Gold
	Straw

Overall Impression:

Pairing Ideas:

Fill wine glasses for
Deliciousness
Rating:

Tasting Notes

Winery _____   Date _____

Name of Wine _____   Vintage _____

Varietal _____   Bottle Price _____

Aroma Notes:	Tasting Notes:

Hint: Use Wine Characteristics Chart

Color:

- Maroon
- Garnet
- Ruby
- Fuchsia
- Salmon
- Peach
- Amber
- Gold
- Straw

Overall Impression:

Pairing Ideas:

Fill wine glasses for Deliciousness Rating:

Tasting Notes

Winery _____ Date _____
Name of Wine _____ Vintage _____
Varietal _____ Bottle Price _____

Aroma Notes:	Tasting Notes:

Hint: Use Wine Characteristics Chart

Color:

Maroon

Garnet

Ruby

Fuchsia

Salmon

Peach

Amber

Gold

Straw

Overall Impression:

Pairing Ideas:

Fill wine glasses for
Deliciousness
Rating:

Tasting Notes

Winery _____   Date _____
Name of Wine _____   Vintage _____
Varietal _____   Bottle Price _____

Aroma Notes:	Tasting Notes:

Hint: Use Wine Characteristics Chart

Color:

- Maroon
- Garnet
- Ruby
- Fuchsia
- Salmon
- Peach
- Amber
- Gold
- Straw

Overall Impression:

Pairing Ideas:

Fill wine glasses for Deliciousness Rating:

Tasting Notes

Winery _____   Date _____
Name of Wine _____   Vintage _____
Varietal _____   Bottle Price _____

Aroma Notes:	Tasting Notes:

Hint: Use Wine Characteristics Chart

Color:

Overall Impression:

Maroon

Garnet

Ruby

Fuchsia

Salmon

Peach

Pairing Ideas:

Amber

Gold

Straw

Fill wine glasses for
Deliciousness
Rating:

Tasting Notes

Winery _____   Date _____
Name of Wine _____   Vintage _____
Varietal _____   Bottle Price _____

Aroma Notes:	Tasting Notes:

Hint: Use Wine Characteristics Chart

Color:

Maroon

Garnet

Ruby

Fuchsia

Salmon

Peach

Amber

Gold

Straw

Overall Impression:

Pairing Ideas:

Fill wine glasses for
Deliciousness
Rating:

Tasting Notes

Winery _____   Date _____

Name of Wine _____   Vintage _____

Varietal _____   Bottle Price _____

Aroma Notes:	Tasting Notes:

Hint: Use Wine Characteristics Chart

Color:

Maroon

Garnet

Ruby

Fuchsia

Salmon

Peach

Amber

Gold

Straw

Overall Impression:

Pairing Ideas:

Fill wine glasses for
Deliciousness
Rating:

Tasting Notes

Winery _____   Date _____
Name of Wine _____   Vintage _____
Varietal _____   Bottle Price _____

Aroma Notes:	Tasting Notes:

Hint: Use Wine Characteristics Chart

Color:

Maroon

Garnet

Ruby

Fuchsia

Salmon

Peach

Amber

Gold

Straw

Overall Impression:

Pairing Ideas:

Fill wine glasses for
Deliciousness
Rating:

Tasting Notes

Winery _____   Date _____

Name of Wine _____   Vintage _____

Varietal _____   Bottle Price _____

Aroma Notes:	Tasting Notes:

Hint: Use Wine Characteristics Chart

Color:

Maroon

Garnet

Ruby

Fuchsia

Salmon

Peach

Amber

Gold

Straw

Overall Impression:

Pairing Ideas:

Fill wine glasses for
Deliciousness
Rating:

Tasting Notes

Winery _____   Date _____
Name of Wine _____   Vintage _____
Varietal _____   Bottle Price _____

Aroma Notes:	Tasting Notes:

Hint: Use Wine Characteristics Chart

Color:

Maroon

Garnet

Ruby

Fuchsia

Salmon

Peach

Amber

Gold

Straw

Overall Impression:

Pairing Ideas:

Fill wine glasses for
Deliciousness
Rating:

Tasting Notes

Winery _____   Date _____
Name of Wine _____   Vintage _____
Varietal _____   Bottle Price _____

Aroma Notes:	Tasting Notes:

Hint: Use Wine Characteristics Chart

Color:

	Maroon
	Garnet
	Ruby
	Fuchsia
	Salmon
	Peach
	Amber
	Gold
	Straw

Overall Impression:

Pairing Ideas:

Fill wine glasses for
Deliciousness
Rating:

Tasting Notes

Winery _____   Date _____
Name of Wine _____   Vintage _____
Varietal _____   Bottle Price _____

Aroma Notes:	Tasting Notes:

Hint: Use Wine Characteristics Chart

Color:

Maroon

Garnet

Ruby

Fuchsia

Salmon

Peach

Amber

Gold

Straw

Overall Impression:

Pairing Ideas:

Fill wine glasses for
Deliciousness
Rating:

CPSIA information can be obtained
at www.ICGtesting.com
Printed in the USA
LVOW04s1036150316

479234LV00020B/298/P